UNCONDITIONAL

Brett C Leonard

BROADWAY PLAY PUBLISHING INC
224 E 62nd St, NY, NY 10065
www.broadwayplaypub.com
info@broadwayplaypub.com

Cover photo by Monique Carboni

I S B N: 978-0-88145-463-5

First printing: December 2010
Second printing: November 2015

Book design: Marie Donovan
Typographic controls & page make-up: Adobe InDesign
Typeface: Palatino
Printed and bound in the U S A

UNCONDITIONAL had its world premiere on 10 February 2008 at New York's Public Theater in a LAByrinth Theater Company production (Artistic Directors Philip Seymour Hoffman and John Ortiz). The cast and creative contributors were:

NEWTON .... Isiah Whitlock Jr
KEITH .... John Doman
JESSICA ....Elizabeth Rodriguez
TRACIE .... Yolanda Ross
SPIKE ....Chris Chalk
LOTTY.. Saidah Arrika Ekulona
GARY..Kevin Geer
MISSY ....Anna Chlumsky
DANIEL ....Trevor Long

Director..Mark Wing-Davey
Assistant director.................................... Scott Illingworth
Scenic design..Mark Wendland
Lighting design .... Japhy Weideman
Sound design.. Bart Fasbender

CHARACTERS & SETTING

NEWTON, *black, 49*
WHITE MAN/DANIEL, *35*
KEITH, *white, late 40s-early 50s*
LOTTY, *black, 40s*
SPIKE, *black, mid-20s*
MISSY, *white, early-20s*
TRACIE, *black, 30s*
JESSICA, *Nuyorican, 30s*
GARY, *white, late 40s-early 50s*

New York City. Present

for Barbara, Bruce, Newton, Willie, Clifton, and Kelvin

with special thanks to
Mark, Phil, John, Bob, David R and David M

ACT ONE

Scene 1

(A dark room)

(The lights should reveal as little as possible—only the necessary information.)

(Willie King's Terrorized *is heard throughout.* NEWTON COLLIER, *forty-nine, African-American, is sitting in an office chair. There's a burning cigarette in his hand. On the back of the chair is a canvas shoulder bag. Under a desk is a green metal waste basket. In front of* NEWTON, *with his back to the audience, is an unrecognizable* WHITE MAN, *standing on a chair. His feet and legs are tied with tape. His arms are taped behind his back. His mouth is gagged and covered.)*

(Around his neck is a noose, attached to an overhead beam.)

(The WHITE MAN *squirms a bit, on and off, occasionally trying to speak, yell, beg.)*

*(*NEWTON *calmly smokes while staring at the* WHITE MAN.*)*

(Eventually, NEWTON *stands.)*

(Pause)

*(*NEWTON *drops his cigarette.)*

(He reaches for something in the darkness. He slowly, calmly unfolds a Confederate Battle Flag, showing it to the WHITE MAN.*)*

(He reaches down and grabs the green metal wastebasket. He approaches the White Man, *stops 3 or 4 steps short, puts the wastebasket on the ground.)*

(He holds the Confederate Flag with one hand, and with the other he pulls a Zippo lighter out of his pants pocket.)

(He lights the Zippo.)

(Pause)

(He sets the flag on fire.)

(He puts the Zippo back in his pocket and holds the flag as it burns.)

(He drops the flag into the wastebasket where it continues to burn.)

(He walks back to the chair and removes a 9mm pistol from the canvas shoulder bag.)

(He approaches the slightly squirming, entirely terrified White Man.*)*

(He stops. Pause)

(He points the gun at the White Man's *face. Pause.)*

(He lowers the gun to his side. Pause)

(He raises the gun once again, pointing it at the White Man's *face. He cocks the gun. Pause)*

(He lowers the gun.)

(He moves to the side and points the gun at the side of the White Man's *head.)*

(He puts the barrel up against the White Man's *temple. He holds it there. He presses the barrel into the side of the* White Man's *head. The* White Man *struggles to stay as still and calm as possible.)*

(The Confederate Flag continues to burn.)

(Willie King continues to sing. His guitar continues to wail.)

(NEWTON *moves to the other side. He presses the barrel against the* WHITE MAN'*s temple.*)

(*Pause*)

(*He removes it.*)

(*He un-cocks the gun and puts it in his waistband, behind his back.*)

(*He takes a pack of Winstons from his shirt pocket, removes a cigarette, returns the pack to his pocket, lights the cigarette with his Zippo. He puts the Zippo back in his pocket.*)

(*He smokes.*)

(*The flag burns.*)

(*Willie King sings.*)

(*He turns and knocks the chair out from under the* WHITE MAN.)

(*The* WHITE MAN *dangles.*)

(*Blackout/silence*)

Scene 2

(*A bar*)

(KEITH L MOORE, *late forties-early fifties, Caucasian, sits on a bar stool with his fifth gin and tonic, but doesn't sound or appear drunk.*)

(*The only other customer at the bar, four bar stools between them, is* LOTTY, *forties, African American. She's had a few herself. And smokes Virginia Slims, using a coffee mug as an ashtray. She doesn't look in* KEITH's *direction. Never. Not a glance. It's as though she doesn't hear a word.*)

KEITH: So this one night a few years back, I'm all fucked-up at this bar after a blow-out at the happy home. I go by myself, as I'm wont to do, an' proceed ta get good n' loaded, nice n' pickled just right—they

finally kick me out. It's a beautiful night for a drive. A
nice drive home ta lovely Teaneck, New Jersey, where
I was livin' at this time. And I'm INTENTIONALLY
swerving all over the road, okay?, from the far left
emergency lane ta the far right shoulder, back n' forth,
for whatever reason—it was a nice night. I run outta
gas. Luckily, I'm on the right hand a' my swerves so I
just sorta roll easy-like onta the shoulder—let the car
come to a stop. I'm fucked. I'm six sheets ta the wind,
I'm outta gas, I spent my last nickel on a goodnight
shot a' Goldschlagger, and I left the house in a huff—
without my wallet, my driver's license, without a
credit card, nada. No I D. So I decide ta PUSH it. I'm
gonna PUSH the car home. I'm like eight miles away.
(Beat) Look, at least you could try ta PRETEND you're
listening. *(Beat)* You're gonna love this part, get a big
kick outta it. So I'm pushing my Pontiac Bonneville
eight miles home ta Teaneck, New Jersey. I got the
car door open, my right hand's on the steering wheel,
my left on the frame a' the car—ya know, where the
door connects with the body—an' I'm makin' like...
like fuckin' ZERO progress, I'm sweatin' like a Zulu,
and what happens but a fuckin' COP pulls over. A
police officer, no partner with'm. Nice enough guy—
young guy, white guy, comes at me with no attitude
or nothin', but still...right? I'm drunk, I don't have
I D, he's sober, he has a GUN, I've been in better
situations. He comes over very helpful-like. He's uh...
this PARTICULAR officer, he's the kind fancies himself
a bit of a Good Samaritan. He does what he does to
protect you and protect me—to protect and serve our
children—to make our streets safe—it's got nothin'
ta do with the fact he dropped outta high school at
fifteen, bought his G E D on the Internet, and failed his
firefighters' physical on six separate occasions. He's
altruistic. He's an American hero. "May I help you,
sir?", he asks. "No thank you, kind officer, but it's

wonderful of you to take the time to care." "Are you
sure? Maybe I could give you a lift or call a tow-truck?"
"Again I thank you, your parents must beam with
pride, but I'd hate to imagine at this very moment,
while others are being carjacked, beaten, and raped,
your services would be wasted on a drunk trying to
push his car home." "Have you been drinking, sir?"
"That's how I got drunk, yes." You still with me,
sweetheart? *(Beat)* Sweetheart?

(No response)

KEITH: So he says, "I want you to think this through
before you answer...are you admitting to me, right
now, that you have been driving this vehicle while
under the influence of alcohol?" "No sir. My FATHER
was a drunk driver. My MOTHER was a mother
AGAINST drunk drivers. Drunk driving is simply
not a part of my life. And HENCE, I decided to PUSH
the car home to AVOID driving drunk—and possibly
killing any late night jaywalkers." *(Beat)* I spent three
days in the can before my wife would bail me out. *(He
sips his drink. He lights a Newport. He uses a coffee mug
as an ashtray.)* Ya know...even more than the fact that
you're black—to be honest—it's the fact that you're
not white. I do not like me the white women. Anything
NON-white really'll usually do me the trick. White
men or white women—I don't like 'em. I'm white. I'm
extremely white. I have freckles and skin tags. I had
melanoma cancer right here on my chest. But I got a
face like Jude Law. Feel free ta glance over at any time.

(No response)

KEITH: I believe all actions have consequences. I believe
all consequences should be ignored if they're gonna
prevent us taking action in the first place. *(Beat)* If I
were to offer to buy you a drink, what would be your
response? What if I offered ta take you home? What

if I offered ta guarantee you the greatest fuck you
ever had? And if in addition, I promised never ta tell
another living soul anything about it? You're wearing
a wedding ring. If you looked over you'd notice I'm
wearing one too. But your husband isn't with you. My
wife hasn't been with me in over six months. Sexually
it's been longer. *(Beat)* You're not a kid anymore. You
have grace and maturity. The way you hold and light
your Virginia Slims. The way you cross your beautiful
legs. The way you know exactly how far your skirt
hikes when you do it. A woman your age knows
what she wants, and what works best for her in the
bedroom. She's not ashamed or embarrassed to ask for
it. I'm no kid myself—I'm man enough to make good
on your requests. I can smell your perfume from here.
Sitting in a shithole like this at almost three o'clock in
the morning, all alone, wearing that kind of perfume.
(Beat) We could remain here as we are, removed
from one another, four bar stools between us, lying
to ourselves why we're here. Or we could take a shot,
be honest, and make each other feel less alone in the
world. Maybe we'll feel like assholes tomorrow, sure,
but for tonight? I'm curious ta find out. I'm right here.
I'm gonna remain right here 'til you decide ta leave
with me or Charlie throws me out. *(Beat)* And if while
you're deciding, you decide you'd like that drink, the
offer still stands. I got money. *(Beat)* I'm Keith. Maybe
later you'll let me know who you are. *(He looks away.
He takes a sip of his drink. He smokes. He stares straight
ahead.)*

*(LOTTY continues to nurse her drink. She smokes. She looks
over at KEITH.)*

(She looks straight ahead once again.)

(Four bar stools between them.)

Scene 3

(Studio apartment)

(SPIKE, mid-twenties, African-American, and his goth-girlfriend MISSY, early twenties, Caucasian.)

(She playfully shakes a gift-wrapped box near her ear in an attempt to figure out what's inside.)

MISSY: A Cadillac Escalade?

SPIKE: No.

MISSY: A home in the Hamptons?

SPIKE: No.

MISSY: Marilyn Manson tickets?

SPIKE: Warmer.

MISSY: An engagement ring?

SPIKE: Much colder.

MISSY: *(Tossing the box to him)* Fuck you.

SPIKE: After you open it, in the ass.

(SPIKE tosses the box back to MISSY.)

MISSY: Mmmm... *(She shakes the box near her ear once again.)*

MISSY: A thousand-gigabyte iPod, a hundred-inch plasma flatscreen, a Blackberry, a subscription to *Blender* —I give up... *(She rips open the package: A 3/4 length black, vinyl jacket with a hood.)* Oh fist me baby, it's beautiful!

SPIKE: I saw that shit, soon as I saw it I was like, nigga, "that's my girl right there, nigga."

(While taking off her clothes:)

MISSY: Dude, it's awesome.

SPIKE: Shit jumped at me, gotchyour name all over that shit.

MISSY: It's expensive though baby, isn't it? *(She continues to strip down to skimpy bra, panties and her knee-high black boots.)*

SPIKE: Expensive, man, fuck the cost, fuck the consequences—this what love's all about, baby.

(MISSY models her new coat.)

MISSY: Whaddaya think?

SPIKE: *(Rubbing his crotch over his baggy jeans)* Mmm, I think some'ns happenin' ta King Cobra.

(MISSY runs over and jumps onto SPIKE's lap, her legs straddling his. They kiss. They stop.)

SPIKE: Happy Birthday, baby.

(MISSY smacks SPIKE across the face.)

MISSY: Sing it, bitch. Sing me my fuckin' birthday song!

(MISSY smacks SPIKE again.)

(He wraps his hands around her neck and begins to choke her.)

MISSY: Fuck yeah, choke me! Sing it motherfucker, sing!!...

SPIKE: *(Sings)* Happy Birthday to you...

MISSY: ...yeah...

SPIKE: ...Happy Birthday to you...

(MISSY spits in SPIKE's face.)

SPIKE: ...Happy Birthday, my Missy...

(MISSY slaps SPIKE.)

(SPIKE spits in MISSY's face.)

MISSY: Fuck yeah!

SPIKE: Happy Birthday to you.

(MISSY *pinches* SPIKE'*s nipples really hard.*)

SPIKE: Mmmphh...

MISSY: Yeah...

(MISSY *pumps her hips faster,* SPIKE *pumps his.*)

SPIKE: ...I love you...

(MISSY *spits in* SPIKE'*s face.*)

SPIKE: ...I love you...

(MISSY *slaps* SPIKE.)

(*Blackout*)

Scene 4

(*A diner*)

(TRACIE, *thirties, African-American and* JESSICA, *thirties, Nuyorican. Coffees and chef salads*)

JESSICA: He raises a finger ta you again, ya hit him with a small appliance ta the side of his fuckin' skull—tell'm run himself into a concrete wall next time he's lookin' for contact. You are nobody's doormat, Tracie—you're not his slave, you're not his geisha, you're not a nanny for the kids—you're his goddamn WIFE. I need more coffee. (*Looking for the waitress, then spotting her*) Lookit this bitch—she out on a cigarette break—you're not eating? (*Sticking her fork into* TRACIE'*s salad*) You gotta eat. (*She eats.*) How you gonna kick the side a' your man's head in if ya got no protein? I hate juss cuz I ask for dressing on the side, that don't mean I only want a teaspoon of it. How's yours, you gonna use yours?... (*She grabs* TRACIE'S *dressing and pours it over her own salad, but never stops talking.*) ...Every time they do this, and by the way—don't think it's coincidence you're black, I'm Puerto Rican—it's a blatant attempt at a subliminal obesity, heart-disease, sickle-cell anemia thing— *(To waitress, who's not in ear shot)*Cunt. *(To* TRACIE*)* Look, there's two kindsa men in this world— Good Men who are Bad Fucks, and Bad Men who're Good Fucks—an' other mothafuckers wouldn't know a good fuck if ya bent 'em over an' fucked 'em in the ass. But sometimes that's exactly what ya gotta do with these limp dicks—ya gotta take CHARGE, that's that. You're in a place—we've all been there—to the "Men are a buncha selfish fuckin' scumbags" place. Their problems are bigger'n yours, their complaints are more valid... *(As she simulates jerking off with the fork:)* ...Blah-blah-blah...Fuck 'em in the mouth. He hits ya again, ya hit'm back, that's that. This dressing sucks. This diner sucks. You shouldn't a' waited three months to tell me this, Trace, I'm your best friend. You wait cuz, why?, cuz you feel sorry for him?, he broke down in tears? Fuck him, he should cry. *(Spots waitress re-entering)* Here go this bitch now—lookit'r—she walk like she got a ironing board stuck up her ass. *(To waitress)* 'Scuse me—yo!—Ironing Board—we need more coffee.

Scene 5

(An office)

(Behind a desk sits DANIEL BREEMS, *thirty-five, Caucasian, on the phone.)*

DANIEL: *(Into phone)* As much as the next guy, right. *(Laughs)* Exactly, hummina-hummina. *(Laughs)* If it's not one thing it's another—just lookit the Japanese. *(Beat)* Like a boomerang—ooo—watch yourself. *(Laughs)*

*(*NEWTON *enters—politely informing* DANIEL *of his presence.)*

*(*DANIEL *motions for* NEWTON *to come in and have a seat.* NEWTON *does.)*

DANIEL: Right, exactly, or "what?", I hear ya. Look, I gotta run, man—no, yeah, no I will, no doubt. No doubt. I look forward to it. *(Laughs)* Okay, yeah, bye-bye. *(He hangs up.)* Sorry, I... Thanks for coming.

NEWTON: You asked ta see me.

(Beat)

DANIEL: You might wanna get the door.

(NEWTON looks to the open door.)

DANIEL: We won't be long I don't think, but...I'd prefer we did this in private.

(NEWTON hesitates, then goes to the door, shuts it, and returns halfway as:)

DANIEL: I called you in here rather than...I wanted to speak to you, one-on-one. Man-to-man. Have a seat.

NEWTON: *(Sitting)* You're makin' me nervous, Mister Breems.

DANIEL: Daniel.

NEWTON: You're makin' me nervous, Daniel.

(DANIEL lifts a manila envelope off his desk and holds it out to NEWTON.)

DANIEL: I'm sorry.

NEWTON: What is it?

DANIEL: It came from headquarters in Tulsa. It wasn't my call.

NEWTON: Tulsa?

DANIEL: In Oklahoma.

NEWTON: I know where it is.

DANIEL: Of course.

(NEWTON takes the envelope. As he opens it and reads the enclosed type-written document:)

DANIEL: Personally, I've been happy with your work and feel you've been a valuable asset to...

NEWTON: ...You've been here three months.

DANIEL: And what I've seen in those three months, my observations, I've...

NEWTON: ...I've been here twenny-five years.

DANIEL: I know.

NEWTON: You know?

DANIEL: You've been here close to twenny-five years.

NEWTON: Twenty-five, Mister Breems...

DANIEL: ...Daniel.

NEWTON: I'm almost fifty years old. How old are you?

DANIEL: I told you it wasn't my call.

NEWTON: How old are you? Please.

DANIEL: I work in Human Resources, Mister Collier.

NEWTON: Newton.

DANIEL: Newton.

NEWTON: Yes.

DANIEL: I'm just the messenger.

NEWTON: Your message sucks.

DANIEL: I agree.

NEWTON: You agree?

DANIEL: I agree.

(Beat)

*(*NEWTON *once again looks at the document.)*

NEWTON: Tulsa, Oklahoma. Shit. *(He tosses the envelope and document onto the desk.)* Why a New York City company got headquarters in Oklahoma in the first place?

DANIEL: There's a few—there's Fort Worth, Boston...

NEWTON: ...It was rhetorical.

DANIEL: Look, Newton, if there's anything I can do...

NEWTON: ...How bout saving me my job?

DANIEL: I meant with regards to references or a letter of recommendation.

NEWTON: I work in H R, too, Mister Breems.

DANIEL: I know. *(Beat)* I know. *(Beat)* The layoffs are severe. There're over thirty-five hundred. More than a hundred an' fifty from the New York office alone. I'm sorry. If there's anything I can do.

NEWTON: This is about my pension, isn't it?

DANIEL: I don't know.

NEWTON: Oh, come on now, Breems, you may be the messenger but I'm three months short a' turnin' fifty, I'm workin' here twenny-five years next month. Twenny-five an' fifty gets me my pension in full. Short a' twenny-five, short a' fifty? I get flat shit. This about money, Mister Breems, you know like I know.

DANIEL: Of course it's about money—I'm gonna have men and women comin' in an' outta here all day, all week, givin' every one the same shit news.

NEWTON: And how many others are comin' up on collecting in full? Bein' cut short one month one end, three months the other? How many a' the thirty-five hundred just happen ta be black?

DANIEL: Is it about race or money, Mister Collier?

NEWTON: How do you differentiate between the two?

DANIEL: Mister Collier...

NEWTON: ...How many are bein' robbed short a' their pensions and what's the percentage that are black?

DANIEL: I'll check if you'd like.

NEWTON: Yeah, I'd like! *(Beat)* I'd like. *(Beat)* I'm sorry I raised my voice.

DANIEL: It's okay. I'm sorry I'm the bearer of such bad news.

NEWTON: Yeah. Thanks.

(DANIEL extends his hand. They shake. NEWTON takes the envelope, turns and heads for the door:)

DANIEL: I'm thirty-five years old.

(NEWTON stops, turns to face DANIEL.)

NEWTON: Thirty-five. You're thirty-five an' I got two daughters I gotta put through college on no pension. This letter says I got two weeks ta clear my office an' get my things. I'm gonna ignore it. I'm gonna be here on my fiftieth birthday, Mister Breems. I'm gonna blow out fifty-one candles, one for good luck. I'll see you around. Thanks for the news. *(He exits.)*

Scene 6

(Starbucks on 125th)

(Over coffee: JESSICA and TRACIE)

JESSICA: Every bully in the world's a big fat pussy underneath. At elementary school when I was growin' up there was this Italian bully kid named Ronnie Mancini who useta beat the shit outta every kid on the playground. The cafeteria, the classrooms, it didn't matter ta this little prick. So one day, there's this kid named Bruce Tompkinson—nerdy, red-hair, freckles, got braces on his teeth an' he's walkin' with those whaddaya call—those two metal walker crutch-type things with the metal arm braces. Totally atrophied legs, all fucked-up, skinny like two chopsticks, but

loose—not chopsticks, like a coupla lo-mein noodles,
and his feet all contorted an' twisted-up-crooked an'
shit, draggin' all behind him an' shit, and he's wearin'
this Cub Scout uniform with lil' tassles an' ribbons on
it—lil' yellow tassles an' pleated shorts, yo, this the
Bronx nineteen-eighty-two—so this Ronnie Mancini,
this Guinea bully kid, he comes up to'm one day—this
gotta be, what, fourth-fifth grade maybe—he's already
terrorized the whole fuckin' neighborhood since
kindergarten—both his uncles an' ol' man are Made
Men on Arthur Avenue, blah-blah-blah—how's your
coffee?—my shit's always cold in this place—they put
a Starbucks in Harlem it's like "fuck 'em, them niggas
don't know from coffee." So this Ronnie the Dago, he
walks over ta lil' crippled Brucie Tompkinson an' he
steals one a' his metal walker thingies, Brucie goes
down, starts crawlin' towards this chain-link fence—
Ronnie Mancini meanwhile he's limpin' around all
retarded-like, makin' fun a' poor lil' Brucie. Nobody
ELSE'S laughin', but Ronnie Mancini can't fuckin'
STOP laughin'—limpin' around, feet draggin' all over
the place—makin' fun a' the physically impaired—
totally fucked up—then Brucie, both arms grabbin'
hold a' the fence, his little crutch danglin'— he comes
sneakin', CREEPIN', like a horror movie Zombie with
flaming red hair, and outta nowhere—outta fuckin'
NOWHERE—with some shit he musta learned in
the Cub Scouts, he takes the OTHER crutch-thing an'
cracks the shit outta Ronnie right to his bully-wop-
dago-fuck-head—whack—right ta the temple—blood
splurtin' all over the place—NOW the other kids start
laughin'—but here's the thing...Ronnie Mancini? This
bully bitch never shows his face around school ever
again—never—that's that. One lil' crack ta the side a'
the brain from a redheaded cripple retarded kid an' the
biggest bully in the Bronx was a bully no more. One
blow, Trace—one shot.

Scene 7

(KEITH's *bedroom*)

(KEITH *and* LOTTY *are in bed.* LOTTY's *head is on his chest, her eyes are closed.*)

KEITH: Lotty? Lotty? Naughty Lotty?

(LOTTY *snuggles closer, eyes shut.*)

KEITH: I, uh... Sweetheart? Can you hear me? Are you sleeping? Sweetheart? *(Beat)* I have chlamydia. You hear? *(Beat)* I lied when I told you I had money. *(Beat)* I like cock. *(Beat)* I'm still in love with my wife. Alright, c'mon, let's go, c'mon—time ta get up. *(He forcefully "removes" her head from his chest.)*

LOTTY: What the fuck?

KEITH: I got a lotta shit I gotta do, I got a full day...

LOTTY: ...So, I got shit too.

KEITH: Terrific, we have lots in common, now let's go.

LOTTY: What kind of asshole are you?

KEITH: The following morning kind, I'm sure I'm not your first.

LOTTY: No, but you're the biggest.

KEITH: Maybe you're right, let's go.

LOTTY: I know I'm right—you don't gotta confirm it for me. I was just tryin' ta get a lil' more sleep, I wasn't tryin' ta fuckin' move in with you.

KEITH: This is the part I was talkin' about, you were warned.

LOTTY: What part?

KEITH: In the bar. The part about we'll feel better at night, but come mornin' we'll feel like a coupla assholes.

LOTTY: I don't feel like an asshole.

KEITH: This's supposed ta be a one night stand, what the fuck're we arguin' about? C'mere, gimme a kiss.

LOTTY: Fuck off.

KEITH: Gimme a big, wet, sloppy one.

LOTTY: I haven't brushed my teeth.

KEITH: The natural odors of a natural woman.

LOTTY: Where's your wife Keith?

KEITH: Why, where's the lil' hubby waitin' for you? At home, on a business trip, the trunk a' your car, maybe?

LOTTY: He's not WAITING for me anywhere— wherever he's at that's just where he happens ta be.

KEITH: C'mon—I haven't brushed my teeth either.

LOTTY: I didn't wanna say nothin', I know.

KEITH: So you gonna kiss me or not?

LOTTY: No.

KEITH: No?

LOTTY: No.

(Beat)

KEITH: Alright, then. Okay.

LOTTY: Okay, what?

KEITH: We'll do it again sometime.

LOTTY: What gives you that idea?

KEITH: Maybe your fingernails still stuck in my back.

LOTTY: Don't flatter yourself.

KEITH: It's more honest than tryin' ta flatter you, sweetheart.

LOTTY: That right?

KEITH: That's correct.

LOTTY: You're a very selfish fuck, Keith.

KEITH: I got money if ya need me ta call ya a cab—so long as you don't live in Newark, or too far up in the Bronx.

LOTTY: Your wife was lucky ta leave you—you're an asshole.

KEITH: You're a forty-plus year old black woman with a pussy the size a' the Panama Canal, you shouldn't be insulting anyone...

LOTTY: ...Comin' from you?!...

KEITH: ...And my WIFE, by the way, isn't LUCKY! You're not LUCKY, I'm not LUCKY, who the fuck do you know that's LUCKY?! All I wanted was ta try an' make you feel a little better for a little while. I know you were able ta do that for me and I thank you, it was nice. And now, here we are in the guilt-ridden, self-loathing ugly part. I'm sorry I insulted you and your pussy—I happen ta like them both—and if there IS a touch a' blame to be had for the occasional slippage, I'll take it, fine, I got a German-Irish dick—but I thought we were more than physically compatible and I had a very lovely time. In addition, I also happen to think you're a very beautiful woman on the OUTSIDE of your vagina as well. And despite the fact that I consider myself LUCKY for the two of us having met, as nice as it was, as nice as you are...you're not my wife, I'm not your husband, besides that little fucked-up fact, it was great ta meet you. *(Beat)* Are you sure I can't give you something for your cab?

LOTTY: I don't live in Newark, Keith. I don't live in the Bronx, either. I don't live in Bed-Stuy, I don't live in Harlem. I live in Westchester, in a mansion, with a half-Olympic size swimming pool, a twelve person jacuzzi and a Wimbledon grass tennis court I've never stepped foot on. I don't NEED your money—but

I'm gonna take it—I had ta put up lissenin' ta your bullshit all night an' all morning and believe me, my physical experience was less enjoyable than yours. Gimme a hundred dollars, I ain't takin' no Yellow, I'm takin' a Limo Town Car—yellow cabs are for low-rent mothafuckers like you.

Scene 8

(SPIKE *and* MISSY'*s studio apartment.)*

SPIKE: *(Offstage)* Baby, I'm sorry, it was a mistake, listen.

(MISSY *enters—desperate, frantic, out-of control. She grabs a piece of aluminum foil and glass pipe. She begins to scrape the foil, trying unsuccessfully to loosen non-existent Meth residue. She unsuccessfully tries to get high—smoking nothing.)*

(SPIKE *enters: the vinyl coat in his hand.)*

SPIKE: I love you. I said I love you!! I'm sorry. Fuckin' sorry!! Baby!! *(He grabs her shoulders as:)* Baby, Relax!

MISSY: Fuck off! *(She runs off, exiting.)*

(SPIKE *follows after as:)*

SPIKE: I had shit on my mind! *(He exits. Offstage)* Happy-fuckin'-birthday!

(Blackout)

Scene 9

(A home office.)

*(*GARY, *late-forties/early-fifties, Caucasian, on the computer.)*

*(*LOTTY *enters, dressed as we saw her at* KEITH's. *She stands in the doorway, looking across the room at her husband.* GARY *ignores her—continues on his computer.)*

LOTTY: Did they get off to school okay?

(No response)

LOTTY: Did you take them or are we supposed to pick them up?

(No response)

LOTTY: *(Growing annoyed)* Did TINA take them or did you?

(No response)

LOTTY: Grow up. *(She turns to exit but is stopped with:)*

GARY: Call your mother.

LOTTY: Mmmph?

GARY: Call your mother.

LOTTY: Is everything alright?

GARY: I'm sure she's fine.

LOTTY: Well, wha'd she say?

GARY: When?

LOTTY: When she called.

GARY: I told you to call HER, I didn't say she called you. Call her and tell her she was right. Tell her you married the wrong man.

LOTTY: Oh, you're so fuckin' dramatic.

GARY: Am I? Am I the dramatic one, dollface? Little Miss Thang? Little Miss...

(LOTTY *calmly flips* GARY *off and exits.*)

GARY: ...I'm not the one who stayed out all night like a two-dollar whore without a phone call!! I'm the one who drove the kids ta school, Dollface! Love of my life! MY "BEST FRIEND"! I'M THE ONE WHO FUCKIN' STAYED HOME WORRYING WHETHER YOU WERE FUCKIN' DEAD OR FUCKIN' ALIVE!!!!

Scene 10

(*A living room*)

(NEWTON *sits in the dark on his well-worn easy-chair. In one hand is a burning cigarette, in the other is a stiff drink.*)

(*Silence*)

(TRACIE *enters. Pause. She approaches from behind.*)

(*Pause*)

(*She kisses the top of his head.*)

(*He doesn't respond or react.*)

(*Pause*)

(*He takes a sip of his drink.*)

(*She walks around, in front of him. She sits on the foot stool.*)

(*Long pause*)

NEWTON: I put the girls ta sleep about an hour ago. We had pizza for dinner.

(*Pause*)

TRACIE: Are you okay? (*Beat*) Baby? (*Pause*) Why are you sitting in the dark for? Mmmph? (*She turns on the*

lamp. Beat) Baby? *(Pause)* It's gonna be okay. *(Pause)*
C'mon, let's get you to bed.

*(TRACIE tries to take the drink from NEWTON's hand. He
forcefully pulls it back.)*

NEWTON: I'm not finished! *(Long pause)* I gave them
mothafuckers twenny-five years of my life. *(Pause)*
Why don't you go in by yourself. *(Beat)* Go on. *(Beat)*
I'll be in in a minute. *(He turns off the lamp.)*

(Pause)

*(TRACIE gets up. She goes to kiss him on the top of his head.
He pulls away.)*

(Pause)

(She moves toward the bedroom.)

NEWTON: Trace?

(TRACIE stops. NEWTON continues to stare straight ahead.)

(Pause)

NEWTON: I'm sorry.

(TRACIE remains—watching her husband.)

(NEWTON remains—seated, staring out, in semi-darkness.)

Scene 11

(JESSICA's apartment.)

*(JESSICA is alone in bed, under the covers. With a remote
control she slowly flips channels on her T V. Flip. Pause.
Flip. Pause. Flip. Pause. Flip. Pause. She turns off the T V
and puts the remote on the bedside table. She puts a retainer
in her mouth. She puts her head on the pillow. She turns off
her bedside lamp.)*

(Blackout)

Scene 12

(KEITH's *apartment*)

(KEITH, *seated at a glass dining table, counts stacks of money. Each stack is bound by a rubber band. Beneath each rubber band is a small piece of yellow legal-pad paper with a hand-printed name and a dollar figure.*)

(*In the middle of the room* SPIKE *practices his golf swing with a 6-iron.*)

SPIKE: You know that nigga only quarter black, right? One quarter, ya know that shit? He half Thai, quarter black, an' quarter white, or Indian, Filipino, some'n. You see this swing, man? Shit is smooth, right? Got me that Vijay swing, look—uggh—poetry—speakin' a black, that nigga Vijay? He darker than I am. Mahatma Vijay. Alright, watch this shit with the putter. Mandingo Vijay. Nigga, you watchin'? Keith—watch me drain this shit.

(SPIKE *has put the 6-iron back in the bag and taken out a putter. He lines up over a ball.* KEITH *is busy re-counting stack after stack of money.*)

SPIKE: Keith? You takin' notes, bro?

(SPIKE *putts the ball toward and into a plastic, green putting machine—the hole catches the ball, then spits it back. Throughout, he continues:*)

SPIKE: Uggh—dead center, baby—never up, never in—like your sex life, right Keith? Keith, you hear me? Never up, never in? I said kinda like your dick, bro— prolly whatchoo do with all that money, huh? Prolly make book so you can buy Levitra, Viagra an' shit, ol' mothafuckah. Yo! Keith! Ai'ght nigga—countchyer lil' money then, I ain' give a fuck—wha' I care- I'm a golfin' nigga—workin' on my game. Twenny-seven feet, uugh, Saint Andrews. (*He misses.*) Shit, you see that? You ain't see shit, nigga—you too busy up in yo' own shit. Fitty feet, Pebble Beach. *(Lines up another)* Ya know, I useta know a girl in high school named Levitra—true story—biggest whore on Campus— prolly mighta even fucked yo' ol' ass, nigga. Where you go ta high school at, huh? Where you go? You like from Vermont or some shit, right? Huh? Yo' ass be like Colorado— Montana, maybe—some white mothafuckah state.

KEITH: I need you to count this with me.

SPIKE: Count what?

KEITH: This stack here.

SPIKE: What about it?

KEITH: I need you ta siddown, shut the fuck up, and count along.

SPIKE: I can't count no better than you.

KEITH: I've counted this stack three times, Spike, and each time I've gotten the same result.

SPIKE: That ain't hard ta do.

KEITH: Put down the club.

SPIKE: I'm workin' on my puttin', though.

KEITH: Siddown.

SPIKE: Which stack you even talkin' 'bout anyway, lemme see...

(SPIKE takes a quick step toward KEITH. KEITH pulls a gun out of the open briefcase, then puts it down in front of him, on the table.)

KEITH: I said put the club away an' sit the fuck down.

SPIKE: Keith, man...

KEITH: ...Siddown.

SPIKE: What the fuck you bringin' out that for, come on man...

KEITH: ...I asked you nicely, I could change my tone if you want. Now sit.

(SPIKE *moves toward the chair, across the table from* KEITH.)

SPIKE: I don't know why you even trippin', bro—bringin' a fuckin' gun out...

KEITH: ...Gimme the putter.

SPIKE: Come on, man...

KEITH: ...Hand me the fuckin' putter.

(KEITH *extends his hand.* SPIKE *hands the putter across the table.*)

KEITH: Now sit.

(SPIKE *sits.*)

SPIKE: You actin' all fucked-up an' shit, bro...

KEITH: ...Shut up. You been talkin' non-stop since you got here.

SPIKE: I had shit I wanted to tell you.

KEITH: About Tiger Woods? I don't give a fuck about Tiger Woods.

SPIKE: You like golf.

KEITH: People talk cuz they got somethin' important ta say or somethin' important to avoid saying. There's nothing important about Tiger Woods.

SPIKE: Lotta mothafuckas disagree wi'that statement right there, Keith—lil' black kids all 'cross America for one—shit, I started playin' cuz a' him—fuckin' OPRAH'S joinin' private golf clubs now—I read about that shit, she joinin' out in fuckin' Santa Barbara—California—black men AND black sistahs joinin' private golf clubs with a buncha white fuckin' JEWS?! That ain't IMPORTANT?! That all TIGER right there, nigga. Now maybe that shit ain't important ta yo' ass, nigga, cuz maybe cuz yo' ass just happens ta be WHITE. Ya see what'm sayin'? You never even thought about that shit like that. I broke that shit down tight, right?

KEITH: Tight.

SPIKE: That nigga for real, Keith, that nigga no joke.

KEITH: Terrific. *(Counting)* One, two, three... I want you to do this with me—out loud, so I can hear you. Three, four...

SPIKE: ...Why you so caught up with this shit—I learned ta count in the third fuckin' grade.

KEITH: Don't make me shoot you, okay? We'll try it again. One. Two.

(KEITH *looks at* SPIKE, *prompting*)

SPIKE: Three.

KEITH: Good. Four.

KEITH & SPIKE: Five. Six. Seven. Eight. Nine. Ten. Eleven. Twelve. Thirteen. Fourteen. Fifteen.

KEITH: I got fifteen. You get fifteen? Mmmph? Spikey? How many'd you get?

SPIKE: Whose stack is that?

(KEITH *pushes a yellow piece of paper across the table.*)

KEITH: It says "Barton—nineteen hundred." Short four. That is your handwriting isn't it?

SPIKE: D'joo count the others?

KEITH: They match.

SPIKE: You count 'em more than once or...

KEITH: ...More than once.

SPIKE: An' they was all good, every one?

KEITH: To the penny.

SPIKE: I dunno, man.

KEITH: What?

SPIKE: I dunno, maybe...

KEITH: ...Maybe what?

SPIKE: Maybe he stiffed you, I dunno.

KEITH: Maybe he stiffed me?

SPIKE: Maybe.

KEITH: Maybe Barton stiffed me?

SPIKE: Why not?

KEITH: Barton? We're talkin' about Barton, Spike.

SPIKE: I don't know WHAT the fuck we talkin' 'bout, bringin' a gun on the table an' shit—shit ain't even got nuttin' ta do with me.

KEITH: You did the collections didn't you?

SPIKE: No, my fuckin' mother did—c'mon man, I dunno what happened—why you all up in my shit for?

KEITH: Would you rather I was up in your mother's shit? Mmmph? Or your lil' punk rock girlfriend's shit? I'll get up in that shit, Spike, gimme the word, "bro", I'd love to.

SPIKE: C'mon, man, that's my girlfriend you talkin' about.

KEITH: Yeah, an' that's my money missing.

SPIKE: That's fucked up an' you know it.

KEITH: Is it?

SPIKE: Talkin' 'bout my mother, talkin' 'bout my girlfriend...

KEITH: ...Where's my four hundred dollars, Spike?

SPIKE: I got no idea.

KEITH: You got no idea?

SPIKE: No.

KEITH: Fifty, seventy-five, I let it go...

SPIKE: ...Relax, bro...

KEITH: ...You're young, you're stupid...

SPIKE: ...I ain't stupid...

KEITH: ...your girl's got a habit...

SPIKE: ... My girl ain't got nothin' ta do with this...

KEITH: ...I SAID TA SHUT THE FUCK UP, NOW SHUT UP! *(Pause)* I like you. I do. I never brought it up before because I understood and I didn't care. Your girl's a drug addict and you're a dumb-ass kid. But now it's four hundred more and you lie to me when I DO bring it up. And you insult me when you lie. Tell me the truth, Spike. Tell me the truth—think long and hard—and look me in my eye.

(Pause)

SPIKE: I was gonna pay you back. Every cent, from the other times, too. I got Missy a vinyl coat. All black, like she like. It's got a hood in it. She loved it, bro. We fucked six times cuz a' that coat. Six times.

(KEITH *grabs the handle of the golf club.)*

SPIKE: That's my heart right there, Keith. She my heart. It was her birthday!

(Blackout)

Scene 13

(DANIEL's *office)*

(DANIEL's *behind his desk, on the phone.)*

DANIEL: *(Into phone)* I'm six-foot-three, well-built, two hundred five pounds, I got tight ab muscles—a nice six pack. I'm twenty-six years of age. I like both older and younger women. I'm well-endowed, a legit nine, with a nice thick head. I like to get to the gym at least four, five times a week. I like poetry. I'm a musician...

(NEWTON *enters.* DANIEL *hangs up.)*

DANIEL: Mister Collier, hello. May I help you?

(NEWTON *puts an 8 1/2 by 11 inch envelope on* DANIEL's *desk.)*

NEWTON: They're papers from my attorney.

DANIEL: Then they should be taken ta legal.

NEWTON: Well I took 'em ta you.

DANIEL: I'll walk 'em over. How you holdin' up?

NEWTON: Don't you wanna know what's inside?

DANIEL: Not really, no.

NEWTON: Why not?

DANIEL: I'm not in legal.

NEWTON: You're inside.

DANIEL: Okay.

NEWTON: You—the entire board of directors: Mister Powell, Mister Robinov—Rich Green—New York, Tulsa, Boston—wrongful firing, race discrimination, age discrimination—I'm not goin' without a fight. This woulda cost y'all a helluva lot less if ya'd just done the right thing from the beginning.

DANIEL: You're preaching to the choir, Mister Collier.

NEWTON: Read the lawsuit, Daniel. I certainly hope it doesn't cause you to lose your job. Me losin' mine? Easy come, easy go, another unemployed black man. But you Daniel? Thirty-five years old, three long months behind your nice, wooden desk. Where would be the justice in that? (*He moves toward the door.)*

DANIEL: This is a big corporation, Mister Collier.

(NEWTON *stops.)*

DANIEL: They'll tie you up so long and cost you so much—you'll lose. *(Beat)* Look—it wasn't my decision to let you go—but it IS my job to tell you about it...I'm sorry. It's my job. The same job you were hoping YOU would get.

NEWTON: And if I HAD I woulda called Tulsa. I woulda gone upstairs—instead of tryin' to save my own ass. I woulda shown those men my file an' I woulda told 'em "this ain't right. This man has worked here for TWENTY-FIVE FUCKIN' YEARS—it ain't right—white, black or otherwise." Instead of tryin' to save my own job. *(Beat)* Have a nice day. Have a nice... goddamn day. *(He exits.)*

Scene 14

(A nice restaurant)

(A table for two)

(A bottle of wine, two wine glasses)

GARY: I'm sorry if I haven't been the greatest conversationalist thus far. I'm better at typing than talking I suppose.

TRACIE: It's okay. The quiet's nice.

GARY: It is kinda, isn't it?

(They sip their wine in silence—the occasional, brief, eye contact.)

(Silence)

TRACIE: What was it about my profile? Why did you respond ta me?

GARY: Your picture.

TRACIE: Yeah?

GARY: I'd be lying if I said I didn't think you were beautiful.

TRACIE: I'm not beautiful.

GARY: I'd be lying if I said I didn't disagree.

TRACIE: I think I'm kinda pretty, sometimes, but...

GARY: ...Well you're wrong. But even so, still...you're doing better than most, believe me. The last time I liked the way I looked was in my photo in my high school year book—when I was a sophomore.

TRACIE: I like the one you posted.

GARY: Well, thank you I suppose, but...

TRACIE: ...That wasn't taken in high school.

GARY: No.

TRACIE: No.

(Beat)

GARY: Neither was yours.

TRACIE: No. *(Beat)* Mine was taken last Christmas.

GARY: As good as it is—the picture?—ta be honest, seeing how you are in person? You oughtta get your money back or retroactively fire the photographer or something—it doesn't do you justice at all. Not even the half of it.

(Beat)

TRACIE: My husband took it.

GARY: Oh.

TRACIE: I have a husband.

(Beat)

GARY: I have an appointment Thursday with an attorney. I'm planning on filing for divorce.

(Pause)

TRACIE: Do you have children?

GARY: No. How 'bout you?

TRACIE: No. *(Beat)* I like this wine.

GARY: I was hoping you would. I'm not really much of a connoisseur, but I...I'm glad. Not too fruity, not too sweet.

TRACIE: It's nice.

GARY: Yeah. It is. *(Pause)* Your husband oughtta be ashamed of himself.

TRACIE: Oh, he's not a professional photographer.

GARY: He oughtta be ashamed of himself for a variety of reasons besides that. He oughtta be ashamed of himself for not knowing where you are right now. For not treating you well enough to make it so you wouldn't want to be here. I don't mean to be bad mouthing a man I've never met. Maybe I should thank him... Here we are, sharing a lovely bottle of wine.

(Pause)

TRACIE: Have you dated many black women before?

GARY: Black and Latina exclusively.

TRACIE: Exclusively, huh?

GARY: *(With a confident shrug)* Well, you know...

TRACIE: Keepin' it real, huh?

GARY: For shnizzy, for shnizoo.

TRACIE: Yeah?

GARY: "Go Tracie, it's your birthday, go Tracie, go Tracie."

TRACIE: "Go Gary, go Gary."

(They both laugh. They're embarrassed. They stop.)

(An awkward silence)

(Then more laughter. And more)

(Then silence once again.)

GARY: Thank you for making me feel comfortable enough to act like an idiot in front of you.

TRACIE: Thanks for making me laugh.

(Pause)

GARY: Is your husband white?

TRACIE: No. *(Beat)* Is your wife black?

GARY: Yes. *(Beat)* I'm keepin' it real, you're movin' on up.

(TRACIE playfully hits GARY.)

TRACIE: Jerk.

GARY: Hey, I'm joking, I'm joking.

TRACIE: You're the one movin' on up, not me.

GARY: Maybe we both are.

(Beat)

TRACIE: Maybe.

(Beat)

GARY: Probably. *(Pause)* Tracie?

TRACIE: Yes?

GARY: When was the last time your husband made love to you? When was the last time he told you how gorgeous you are? When's the last time you believed him when he told you he loved you? When's the last time you believed it without him having to say anything? *(Pause)* I'm extremely attracted to you, Tracie. And I wonder how you feel about me.

(Pause)

TRACIE: When's the last time you made love with your wife?

GARY: I don't remember.

TRACIE: I don't remember the answers to any of your questions. I don't have answers anymore. I haven't had answers in a long time. I haven't been happy in a long time. I'm happy you liked my profile. I'm happy I decided to respond. I'm happy I'm sitting here across from you right now. I'm happy right now. It's been a long time, Gary. It's been a very long time.

Scene 15

(NEWTON's office)

(Charles Caldwell's Old Buck blares—starting at the 1:15 mark.)

(Two white men in ski-masks vandalize NEWTON's office.)

(They unfurl a Confederate Flag and drape it over NEWTON's desk.)

(They hang an eight-knot hangman's noose from an overhead beam.)

(On a wall they spray paint: "THE SILENT NIGGER LIVES, THE LOUD NIGGER DIES", "A GOOD NIGGER'S A DEAD NIGGER".)

Scene 16

(KEITH's apartment)

(SPIKE is on the floor—beaten and bloody. Barely breathing. Blood has spattered onto KEITH'S face and shirt.)

(The bent, crooked, bloody golf club is on the floor.)

KEITH: I hope your girlfriend enjoys her new coat. I hope she sleeps in it. I hope she appreciates what you've done. She won't. She won't, Spike. But it would be goddamn nice if she did. Why the fuck didn't you just ask?!

Scene 17

(NEWTON's office)

(Lights up on NEWTON's vandalized office as we hear Otis Taylor's "Feel Like Lightning"—from the beginning of the song.)

(NEWTON stands in the doorway.)

(He looks to the noose. To the graffiti. To the Confederate Flag. To the books and papers strewn about the floor.)

(He stands frozen. He takes it in.)

(Pause)

(He enters.)

(He takes the flag off the desk. He folds it.)

(He picks up a chair that's been knocked over. He moves it to the hanging noose.)

(He stands on the chair. He unties the rope from the overhead beam.)

(He gets down from the chair.)

(He sits in it.)

(He looks around.)

(He stares straight ahead, the noose in his hands.)

(Eventually—the lights and music fade to silence and black.)

END OF ACT ONE

ACT TWO

Scene 1

(Donny Hathaway's "A Song for You" is heard as lights slowly rise to reveal NEWTON.)

(Alone)

(In his easy chair)

(A cigarette burns in the ashtray. A stiff drink is in his hand. He doesn't drink from it. He doesn't smoke the cigarette. He sits motionless—staring straight ahead in a dimly-lit, smoke-filled room.)

(Music continues and lights remain on NEWTON *as: a soft, warm light slowly rises on* GARY *in a hotel room. He is seated on the foot of a king-sized bed. He wears slacks—but no shoes, no socks, an unbuttoned shirt.)*

*(*TRACIE *enters [from the bathroom]. She wears a black negligee. She stops. She stands nervously.)*

*(*GARY *rises, facing her.)*

(They stare at each other.)

(They approach.)

(They stop a foot or two apart.)

(Pause)

(He reaches out a hand and gently takes one of hers.)

(She reaches out her other hand and takes one of his.)

(They slowly lean into one another. A kiss. And another. And another)

(He runs the back of his hand along her cheek, down her neck, onto her shoulder, kissing each body part as he goes.)

(He moves the strap of her negligee off her shoulder. She moves it back.)

(He kisses her neck. Then her mouth.)

(She kisses him back.)

(Their kissing becomes passionate.)

(And more passionate.)

(The music fades to silence.)

(She pulls away.)

TRACIE: I can't, please, I...

(GARY stops.)

TRACIE: I'm sorry. *(Beat)* I want to.

GARY: It's okay.

(Pause)

TRACIE: My husband slapped me.

GARY: I'm sorry.

TRACIE: You're sorry?

GARY: Yes.

(Beat)

TRACIE: Three months ago. *(Beat)* He won't let me forgive him.

GARY: We can go if you'd like.

TRACIE: I don't know what I'm doing.

GARY: Neither do I.

(Beat)

TRACIE: Hold me? *(Beat)* Okay? *(Beat)* Hold me.

(He does.)

TRACIE: Tighter?

(He does.)

TRACIE: Tell me I'm beautiful.

GARY: You're beautiful.

TRACIE: Kiss me.

(He does.)

TRACIE: Again.

(He does.)

TRACIE: Again.

(He does.)

TRACIE: Again.

(He does.)

TRACIE: Again.

(They kiss.)

(They go to the bed. The "petting" becomes heavier, he kisses her breasts.)

(She stops him.)

TRACIE: Hold me.

(He does.)

TRACIE: Just hold me.

(He does.)

(Donny Hathaway's "A Song for You" begins once again [at the 2:47 mark].)

(Lights remain on TRACIE and GARY in bed, as they embrace.)

(Lights remain on NEWTON...in his easy chair, staring straight ahead, drink in hand, burning cigarette in the ashtray.)

(As the song continues, lights rise on LOTTY, *at home, alone, smoking a Virginia Slim, reading a magazine. She glances at a bedside digital clock.)*

(Lights rise on JESSICA, *alone, in bed, under the covers, blankly staring at a flickering television screen.)*

(Lights rise on DANIEL, *alone, on his bed, sitting up, reading a James Lee Burke novel.)*

(Lights rise on MISSY, *alone, on the fold-out sofa-bed. She puts a cigarette out on her arm. She smokes crystal meth.)*

(Lights on KEITH *and* SPIKE. KEITH *sits at the glass table.* SPIKE *is bloody and motionless on the floor.)*

*(*SPIKE's *cell phone rings. Music stops.)*

(Five rings)

(Silence)

(The ringing begins once again. Ring. Ring. Ring. Ring. Ring. Then stops.)

*(*DANIEL *dials his phone, then pushes a series of buttons.)*

DANIEL: *(Into phone)* Hey, um, hey...this is uh...this is Steve, I'm...I'm callin' pretty late here, it's...it's comin' up on three-thirty almost...I can't sleep, so...I'm just looking to have a little conversation. Maybe meet at some point. I'm callin' outta New York—Manhattan— the Upper West Side. I'm thirty-two years old. I'm six-feet tall. I'm single. I'm recently divorced. It's only been official now less than four months, I'm...I'm just looking for conversation, I...I wanna talk. I'm a good listener, too. *(Beat)* I'm lonely. *(Beat)* Connect if you're interested. Thanks. *(He presses a button on the phone and waits.)*

*(*JESSICA *turns off the T V. She looks at her digital clock.)*

*(*LOTTY *dials her phone.)*

LOTTY: *(Into phone)* It's me again. It's almost four. Just... call me back, okay? I won't answer, I won't pick up. Just...leave a message. Lemme know you're alright. *(She hangs up.)*

(KEITH rises from the table. He exits.)

(JESSICA picks up the phone. She looks at a small piece of paper. She dials. She waits. She presses a few buttons.)

JESSICA: *(Into phone)* Hi. *(Beat)* I'm Jessica. *(She removes the retainer from her mouth.)* This is my first time calling. *(Beat)* I don't know WHY I'm calling really, I... *(Beat)* Thanks. *(She pushes a button on her phone. She waits.)*

(KEITH enters with a bucket, mop, and shower curtain. He leans the mop against the table.)

(He lays the shower curtain on the floor.)

(LOTTY smokes a Virginia Slim.)

(MISSY smokes meth.)

(NEWTON stares straight ahead.)

(TRACIE and GARY sleep in one another's arms.)

(KEITH rolls SPIKE onto the shower curtain. He begins mopping blood.)

(JESSICA presses a button on her phone.)

(DANIEL presses a button on his phone.)

DANIEL: *(Into phone)* Hello?

JESSICA: *(Into phone)* Steve?

DANIEL: This is Steve.

JESSICA: Hi.

DANIEL: Hi.

JESSICA: This is Jessica.

DANIEL: Hey.

JESSICA: Hey.

(Pause)

DANIEL: Wow.

JESSICA: What?

DANIEL: Nothing, no, I... Hey.

JESSICA: Hey.

DANIEL: I'm glad we connected.

JESSICA: I'm not sure yet. I'll let ya know.

DANIEL: Fair enough.

(Pause)

JESSICA: Divorce sucks, right?

DANIEL: You too, huh?

JESSICA: About two years now. It gets easier.

DANIEL: I'm alright, I guess.

JESSICA: Better than a shitty marriage, right?

DANIEL: I guess.

JESSICA: Guess? C'mon, loneliness is loneliness, we all know what that is, but you still feel it's gonna come to an end, ya know? Ya see fat ugly baldheaded people holdin' hands all the time, in public even, so ya gotta figure, shit, right? I gotta meet somebody sometime, but, yeah, I know what ya mean...when you're IN that marriage? A shitty marriage, nasty shitty, I hate you, I hate your body, your face, your entire fuckin' FAMILY shitty—I agree—it's like you're NEVER gettin' out— like prison, right Steve? *(Beat)* Steve? *(Beat)* You still there?

DANIEL: I'm here.

JESSICA: I thought I mighta ran you off maybe.

DANIEL: Nuh-uh.

JESSICA: No?

DANIEL: No.

JESSICA: Oh. *(Beat)* That's cool.

(As LOTTY *exits [offstage].)*

DANIEL: I like your voice, Jessica.

JESSICA: My voice?

DANIEL: Yeah.

JESSICA: What about it?

DANIEL: I dunno. I like the way it sounds. *(Beat)* You live in New York?

JESSICA: Yeah.

DANIEL: Me too.

JESSICA: I know—Upper West Side, right?

DANIEL: Right.

JESSICA: Where're you from originally, you don't sound like New York.

DANIEL: Originally, Oklahoma. I moved here about fifteen years ago—to go to N Y U.

JESSICA: That's a good school, right?

DANIEL: It was alright.

JESSICA: Where do you live on the Upper West Side? You live OLD Upper West or NEW Upper West? I know bitches up in INWOOD talkin' 'bout they live NEW Upper West—Washington Heights—Dominican mothafuckas mostly—white Columbia students, too— real estate brokers sell it like that—"welcome to the NEW UPPER WEST SIDE, 163rd and Broadway"— welcome ta puttin' families been there fifty years out on the fuckin' street—senior citizens too, wha'do they care?—they got wheelchairs, Steve—fuck 'em, put 'em on the street, that's that—gentrifyin' greedy lil' pricks. *(Beat)* Hello? *(Beat)* Steve?

DANIEL: You got a little anger in ya, don't ya Jessica?

JESSICA: *(Apologetic, soft, almost child-like)* Maybe.

DANIEL: Maybe?

JESSICA: A little.

DANIEL: Just a little, huh?

JESSICA: Sometimes.

DANIEL: Yeah?

JESSICA: Sometimes. *(Beat)* I got a lotta other stuff in me too, though.

DANIEL: Like what?

JESSICA: I dunno.

DANIEL: Sure you do. Tell me. What's inside?

(Beat)

JESSICA: No.

DANIEL: No?

JESSICA: Not yet.

(TRACIE wakes. She sits on the edge of the bed. She looks at GARY. He doesn't stir.)

(KEITH sits at the table, staring at SPIKE.)

DANIEL: The OLD Upper west. Seventy-eighth and Amsterdam.

JESSICA: That's nice there.

DANIEL: Yeah.

JESSICA: I bet that means you got a good job then, right?

DANIEL: Right.

JESSICA: Don't tell me you're in real estate.

DANIEL: No. The airlines.

(TRACIE exits [offstage] as:)

JESSICA: You get free travel? My friend's husband works for the airlines, but they never go anywhere, I think maybe Disneyworld once.

DANIEL: Where do you wanna go?

JESSICA: Wha' do you mean?

DANIEL: Where can I take you? Yes—I get free travel. Where do you wanna go?

(Beat)

JESSICA: I dunno.

DANIEL: Go on. Tell me where you've never been.

(NEWTON drinks.)

(GARY wakes. He looks beside him. No one.)

DANIEL: Jessica? You still there?

(MISSY rocks back and forth, knees wrapped in her arms.)

(NEWTON drinks.)

(KEITH smokes.)

DANIEL: Hello?

JESSICA: That's good you got a good job, I think. It gives a man dignity, ya know? Not his IDENTITY, but... his dignity. Knowing he DOES something. Knowing others DEPEND on him. Only thing you could depend on my Ex for was ta piss his pants on a three day drunk. Thank God we didn't have kids, right? *(Beat)* You got kids, Steve?

DANIEL: No.

JESSICA: Just make everything more complicated. Make it harder ta walk away.

DANIEL: Probably.

JESSICA: Definitely. Much harder.

DANIEL: Yes. Much.

(GARY looks toward the bathroom. He sees the light, he hears the sink. He's happy.)

JESSICA: Hey... You wanna know something?

DANIEL: What?

JESSICA: I like your voice too.

DANIEL: Yeah?

JESSICA: Yeah.

DANIEL: I'm glad we connected, Jessica. *(Beat)* Hello?

JESSICA: Why's that?

DANIEL: I dunno. I just am. I feel better.

JESSICA: You do?

DANIEL: I do.

JESSICA: Good. That's good. Me too.

(Lights to black on everyone and everything...except NEWTON.)

(TRACIE enters, quietly—her high-heels in her hand.)

(She starts to move for the bedroom.)

(Before she can exit:)

NEWTON: You shoulda called. *(Beat)* Just that you were all right. *(Beat)* Not ta worry.

(Pause. She begins to move once again.)

NEWTON: I know where you were, Trace.

(She stops.)

NEWTON: Jessica called three times. Sayin' she couldn't getchyou on your cell. I couldn't get you either. *(Beat)* I told the girls you were with Jessica. But then Jessica? Well, she calls here. Our daughters, Trace...they asked me where their mother was. They wanted me ta call the police, and the hospitals. Worrying about their mom. I lied. I told 'em you called earlier an' I forgot.

That you told me you were with Aunt Cheryl for a surprise party at her work. In case they ask.

(She moves again.)

NEWTON: What color was he, Trace? What race was this man?

(She stops. Beat)

NEWTON: I'm not mad. It's a question. Your black man lost his job. He raised his hand. What color was he, Trace—when your black man fulfilled their cliche?

(Pause)

TRACIE: I should've called. *(Pause)* He was black. *(Beat)* Goodnight. *(She exits.)*

(NEWTON continues to stare straight ahead. He takes a sip of his drink.)

(Cross fade:)

(Lights slowly down to black on NEWTON as they rise on the following:)

Scene 2

(KEITH's apartment)

(SPIKE's cell phone is ringing.)

(KEITH moves to SPIKE.)

(He reaches into SPIKE's pockets.)

(KEITH takes SPIKE's cell phone out of SPIKE's jeans.)

(The ringing stops. KEITH puts the phone on the table. He turns to exit.)

(The ringing begins again. KEITH turns back and answers the phone.)

KEITH: *(Into phone)* Hello. No, this is...listen, no!...no! —
MISSY!? —He can't, he, listen!... Will you shut the fuck
up, shut up! *(Beat)* It's about Spike.

Scene 3

(GARY's home office.)

*(GARY, home from his night with TRACIE, is at his
computer.)*

*(LOTTY enters [dressed as we've seen her thus far in ACT
TWO].)*

LOTTY: I left you three hundred fuckin' messages!

GARY: Aren't we in the mood for exaggeration?

LOTTY: I CALL, Gary—when I'm out, I fuckin' call!

GARY: Do you?

LOTTY: Fuck you!

GARY: We don't fuck, remember? I mean, YOU
fuck...other people you fuck, but WE? I'm busy
on my computer, Lotty...I'm sorry I kept you up
unnecessarily, everything is perfectly splendid and in
order, you may go back to sleep now.

*(GARY starts to type. LOTTY yanks the keyboard off the
desk.)*

LOTTY: We have RULES, Gary!! We have fuckin' rules!!

GARY: You didn't call! Not the other night, you didn't!

LOTTY: I called.

GARY: No you didn't.

LOTTY: I FUCKIN' called!

GARY: You didn't.

LOTTY: Did to.

GARY: Did not.

LOTTY: Did to.

GARY: Did not.

LOTTY: Well get USED TO IT, then—I didn't call, I didn't call, maybe I did, maybe I didn't.

GARY: You didn't.

LOTTY: Fine, I didn't, fuck you, I didn't, an' from now on I won't. I hope you're fuckin' happy.

GARY: I am happy! I met a woman, Lotty—a spectacular woman—and the best thing about her is she isn't you. Now gimme back my keyboard—I wanna finish telling her goodnight.

LOTTY: Fuck her! *(She smashes the keyboard to the floor.)* Tell your CHILDREN goodnight!

(Blackout as Otis Taylor's Boy Plays Mandolin *is heard [Starting at 1:57 mark] as lights rise on:)*

Scene 4

(TRACIE's/NEWTON's bedroom.)

(TRACIE is in bed. Eyes closed.)

(Music continues.)

(NEWTON enters.)

(He slowly approaches. Drunk. Uneasy on his feet and in his mind.)

(He stands over her.)

(She doesn't stir.)

(He reaches out a hand, toward his wife, as though to touch her head.)

(He hesitates. He does not touch her.)

(He drops his hand to his side.)

(Pause)

(He turns and slowly walks away.)

(She opens her eyes.)

(He exits.)

(She looks towards the door.)

(Blackout/silence)

Scene 5

(KEITH's *apartment)*

MISSY: It was my birthday...we were gonna fuck each others' brains out ta celebrate, ya know...but he got carried away or...he was someplace else...he juss...kept going and going—I couldn't breathe, he was choking me harder and harder. I said "diamonds", his hands around my neck. You couldn't hear. I tried to push him off, I started hitting him, punching him in the chest and his face. He stops and looks at me, lost, no idea, he has no idea what just happened. His mind was... He never said anything? You're his friend.

KEITH: No.

MISSY: He bought me this coat—for my birthday. It's nice, right? *(Beat)* It looks good on me? *(Beat)* Keith? *(Beat)* It looks good?

KEITH: Yeah.

MISSY: Yeah?

KEITH: You look great.

MISSY: Do I?

KEITH: You're beautiful.

MISSY: You didn't call the police, did you? I don't wanna talk ta no police.

KEITH: No.

(Desperately, unsuccessfully searching through her bag, her pockets, dropping stuff onto the floor as...)

MISSY: ...Fuck-fuck-fuck-fuck, do you have a uh, a, a, FUCK FUCK FUCK FUCK!!...

(KEITH grabs MISSY, tries to control her, but she continues saying "fuck" and trying to hurt herself.)

KEITH: Listen to me—Missy, stop, knock it off—listen—LISTEN—SHUT THE FUCK UP! *(He grabs her face.)* SHUT UP!

(MISSY stops. KEITH holds her arms firmly.)

MISSY: I was gonna get'm diamonds for HIS birthday.

(KEITH releases his grip.)

MISSY: Earrings, ya know? I'd been saving, I... *(She approaches SPIKE.)* "Diamonds, baby. All ya gotta do is say 'diamonds'—that'll make me stop anything." He was supposed ta stop.

KEITH: I know.

MISSY: He was supposed ta fuckin' stop, he was supposed ta stop, Keith... *(She begins to hit SPIKE's dead body.)* ...he was supposed ta fuckin' stop!...

(Throwing MISSY to the ground, away from SPIKE:)

KEITH: ...Knock it off...

MISSY: ...Fuck me, Keith, will you fuck me, fuck me...

KEITH: ...Cut it out, stop...

MISSY: *(Grabbing at his belt)* ...Fuck me, please, fuck me, Keith...

KEITH: ...Missy...

MISSY: *(Pulling down her pants)* ...I need you to fuck me, will you fuck me...

KEITH: ...Stop—Missy!...

MISSY: ...Fuck me while I kiss him goodbye, fuck me, please...

KEITH: *(Grabbing her firmly)* ...Knock it off, MISSY!, STOP!!...

MISSY: *(Breaking down, calm)* Please... Please, Keith? Please?

(KEITH holds MISSY's arms. He looks her in the eyes.)

KEITH: I'm not gonna call the police. We can't tell anyone. Do you understand? We need to keep this to ourselves. Whoever did this... Okay? ...It will be taken care of. You understand? *(Beat)* Missy?... Do you understand?

(MISSY nods, she understands.)

KEITH: Good. *(He pulls up her pants.)* When he got here... you were the only thing he talked about. How much he loved you. How he wanted me to make sure you know.

MISSY: I said "diamonds" but he wouldn't stop.

KEITH: I know.

MISSY: I never told'm I loved him.

KEITH: Tell him now.

MISSY: I can't.

KEITH: Tell him now, Missy.

MISSY: I can't!

(KEITH uncovers SPIKE's face as:)

KEITH: Tell him you love him.

MISSY: I can't.

(KEITH grabs MISSY and forces her down. He pushes her face into SPIKE.)

KEITH: Tell'm you love your new coat. Tell'm you forgive him. Tell'm you love him, Missy. Tell him how much you love him.

MISSY: *(To SPIKE)* I love you. I love you. I love you, I love you, I love you...

(Lights fade...)

(...as R L Burnside's Stole My Check *blasts.)*

(The song cuts to silence as:)

Scene 6

(DANIEL's office)

(NEWTON slams photos onto the desk.)

(DANIEL is seated on the other side.)

NEWTON: "The Silent Nigger Lives, The Loud Nigger Dies"! "A Good Nigger's a Dead Nigger"!!

(From out of his shoulder bag comes the Confederate flag.)

NEWTON: A Confederate-mothafuckin'-Flag! *(And then the noose)* An eight-knot noose—eight knot—that a threat a' goddamn MURDER—eight knot snap a mothafucka neck three times my size! "The Silent Nigger Lives, The Loud Nigger Dies"?! Who the nigger, Mister Breems?! You the nigger? Huh? You the nigger, Daniel?! CUZ I AIN'T NO GODDAMN NIGGER! What happens I'm in that office when they do this?! I got two daughters, Daniel!! I got two little girls. This ain't my pension no more, this the color a' my goddamn skin! And this here New York!! This New York goddamn City, this ain't no Birmingham, ain't no Selma in the Sixties—this the right here, right now, mothafucka, an' whatchyou gonna do about it?!

Whatchyou gonna do, Daniel? I don't want no tied-up lawsuit dead-ends, death threats—I want justice! I want my goddamn job! We gonna call Tulsa, Dan. Pick up the phone. Pick it up.

DANIEL: It's after hours, Mister Collier, there's nobody there...

NEWTON: ...Tulsa's an hour behind, pick up the phone.

DANIEL: But it's past eight here, so out there it means...

(NEWTON *pulls the 9MM from his bag—scaring himself as much as* DANIEL.)

NEWTON: ...I said pick up the phone. Pick it up.

DANIEL: Newton...

NEWTON: ...An' when we're through I want YOUR job. Not "NO" job—your job. Y'all had a choice from the beginning. Pick up that goddamn phone!

DANIEL: I need you to CALM DOWN, Mister Collier.

NEWTON: ...WHAT?!

DANIEL: You need to calm down and take a breath.

(NEWTON *pistol-whips* DANIEL.)

(*Blackout*)

Scene 7

(*A diner*)

(JESSICA *and* TRACIE)

(TRACIE *is eating.* JESSICA *is not—coffee only.*)

JESSICA: We were on for more than an hour—women call free—we didn't exchange numbers, not yet, but...

TRACIE: ...Not YET?

JESSICA: Yeah, YET.

TRACIE: I see.

JESSICA: Our talk flowed, Trace, where he's from, where he lives, stuff about my life—I'm goin' out with this guy—we already made plans.

TRACIE: No you didn't.

JESSICA: Did to—white boy from Oklahoma.

TRACIE: From a chat line?

JESSICA: Why, you want the number?

TRACIE: No thanks.

JESSICA: I'll hold on to it for ya. I'm about ta date a white guy from Oklahoma named Steve. You ever been with a white guy? You gone white, Trace?

TRACIE: Nuh-uh, no.

JESSICA: Could be 'the one', ya never know—could be fulla shit too—how he looks, bad breath, broke-ass-in-debt—but I got a good feeling, Trace—I BETTER—I'm a no-longer-eighteen-year-old bank teller with about two-an'-a-half eggs left. You got kids, you got Newton. I got assholes on the subway, I got an asshole ex-husband and I got that asshole cheatin' ex-boyfriend still working with me side-by-side at the bank. We don't even look at each other.

TRACIE: One of you's gotta get a new job.

JESSICA: I was there first! This new guy, Steve? He works for the airlines like Newt. He asked me "Where can I take you, Jessica?" You heard? "Where would you like to fly away with me?" We're gonna start he takes me ta dinner. Then I figure Cancun's suppose ta be nice.

TRACIE: Hawaii too.

JESSICA: Wherever—outta New York, somewhere warm—Anguilla maybe.

TRACIE: Angueela?

JESSICA: Anguilla. I looked it up online after we hung up—white sand, blue water, brown skin. You got your appetite back.

TRACIE: A little.

JESSICA: We'll order dessert—you like pumpkin pie or sweet potato?

TRACIE: Either one.

JESSICA: I want a family, Trace. I need to HEAR things and FEEL things... Where's our waitress? I swear to God we're never comin' here again. From now on it's Five-Star-Zagat-Guide, candlelight, warm weather, you, me, Newt and Oklahoma Steve—yee-haw! *(Raising her coffee mug in a toast)* To Anguilla.

TRACIE: *(Raising her coffee mug)* To Anguilla.

JESSICA: I need more coffee!

Scene 8

(The bar)

(KEITH's seated on his regular stool.)

(LOTTY's at the bar.)

(Four barstools between them)

(They look out, straight ahead.)

LOTTY: This time we play by MY rules. You do what I say. We go where I say we go. Not your place, not mine. I got a room. It's a shithole. There's nothing nice or fancy or high-class about it. It smells like roach spray and dead rat. I picked it out special just for you.

Scene 9

(DANIEL's *office*)

(DANIEL *is seated—his torso and arms are tied to the chair with the rope [the noose].*)

(NEWTON *digs through filing cabinets and drawers. He finds a gym bag. He pulls out a tee-shirt, socks, sweatshirt, sweatpants, boxing wraps and a towel. He dumps the items onto the desk. He finds scotch tape, multiple rolls.*)

(*He secures* DANIEL's *feet and legs.*)

(*The door has been secured with the desk, a chair, the lock. The gun is in his waistband. He double-checks the security of the door.*)

(DANIEL *speaks throughout:*)

DANIEL: I'm from Oklahoma, yes, but not Tulsa—I'm from Edmond, a suburb outside Oklahoma City—I've been in New York more than seventeen years. My father's a liberal Democrat defense attorney FAMOUS, Mister Collier, famous in Oklahoma for his Pro-Bono work in and around the community, primarily the African-American community. My mom's a grade-school teacher in the public school system in downtown Oklahoma City—my brother's married to a Mexican girl, for chrissake. What happened with your JOB, what happened with your OFFICE, it's reprehensible, Mister Collier—unacceptable and repugnant—and despite having zero involvement in either event—ZERO, Mister Collier, I repeat—I had NOTHING to do WITH, nor any knowledge OF—yet I'm willing, right here, to accept responsibility— whatever you want—for the idiotic, hateful doings of misguided members of my so-called race—I apologize! And I accept whatever you want—you want phone calls, letters—my own resignation?! We can prosecute to the fullest extent of the law—I'll access the security

tapes from the hallway outside your office—I'll ask my
father for help—but if you continue down this road,
please, if you continue...nothing good, Mister Collier,
please...I'm sorry...plea...

(NEWTON *gags and tapes* DANIEL's *mouth.*)

Scene 10

(*An upscale hotel room*)

(GARY *and* TRACIE)

(*They dance slowly, in one another's arms, to Lizz Wright's
cover of "A Taste of Honey"- from the beginning of the
song.*)

(*A full minute*)

(*Lights remain on* GARY *and* TRACIE *as:*)

(*Lights rise on* JESSICA—*in a nice restaurant—all dolled-up
and beautiful—alone at a table for two—waiting for her date
with* STEVE *[*DANIEL*].*)

(*Lights remain on* JESSICA, GARY *and* TRACIE *as lights rise
on:*)

(*A dive shithole motel room.*)

(LOTTY *and* KEITH *fuck. Hard, impersonal. Doggy-style, no
eye-contact.*)

(*Between grunts and groans they repeat, again and again,
almost to themselves:*)

KEITH: [Diamonds, diamonds, diamonds, diamonds...]

LOTTY: [Yes, yes, yes, yes, yes...]

(JESSICA *waits for her date.*)

(GARY *and* TRACIE *dance.*)

(KEITH *and* LOTTY *fuck.*)

Scene 11

(DANIEL's office)

(DANIEL is bound, tied and gagged. He stands on the chair with the noose around his neck—as we saw him in the opening scene of the play.)

(NEWTON is now calm, collected.)

NEWTON: I don't KNOW you were involved with my dismissal. The extent of your exact participation. Nor to the destruction and threats in my office. I don't KNOW. And I don't care. And more importantly, YOU don't care. Despite your protestations and your White-Guilt-obsessed Mommy an' Daddy and Mexican sister-in-law—with all due respect, Daniel—you're fulla shit. You hate me like I hate you. When you're alone in the privacy of your own mind—you hate me. And you're afraid. As politically incorrect as that may sound to a "left-wing-liberal" such as yourself—we scare you. I scare you. My rage. My ignorance. My history. My dick. You're terrified. You don't LIKE that you are—in fact you DISLIKE it, I know—which only makes you like YOURSELF less too—bad on top a' bad. Don't worry, I won't tell anyone. But be honest, Daniel—be honest: If your sister—or daughter—or your mom, the Democratic schoolteacher—one a' them brings home a man with skin the color a' my own—what would you THINK, Daniel? Mmph? What would you THINK? Not, what would you SAY? Or DO? But THINK? (Beat) How would you feel on their wedding day? (Beat) On the birth of the little black babies? (Beat) It's okay. If it makes you feel any better, I use to feel the same way. Full a' fear and terror. And I hated my mother for all of it. For instilling in me "be kind,""be polite," "be invisible". "Don't be a Bad Nigger, Newt. No one likes a Bad Nigger." She was trying to PROTECT me, and I forgive her. But I don't forgive you. I hate you. I've hated you my entire life. But I listened ta my mom an' played nice—shuckin' an' jivin', singin' "Kum-ba-yah-God-love-the-white-man-cuz-the-white-man-love-me." No more. Today I behave on the outside how y'all always made me feel on the inside. I'm right here. I'm not invisible. *(Beat.)* I'm the last thing you're ever gonna see.

(NEWTON *remains still, calm, smoking his cigarette.* DANIEL *struggles.)*

(Lights to black)

Scene 12

(Upscale hotel room)

(TRACIE *holds a diamond ring in a ringbox.)*

GARY: You don't have to answer. I know it's insane, it's absurd and impulsive—I know, and I don't care—I've never been impulsive in my life. I've never felt like this, Tracie, I'm... I'm usually rigid, I'm organized... I'm even boring most of the time, but I don't feel boring with you, I... I just don't. Listen, I... Okay...I don't KNOW that you're the ONE—I don't KNOW that. One can never really KNOW. But I do know my wife ISN'T. And I don't believe your husband is either, for you. I'm different with you, Tracie. I'm happy. Me. You make me feel good about being ME. I never feel good about being me, and... and I believe I do the same for you. I've never been so sure of anything in my life. Tell me you disagree and I'll leave you alone. I promise. I'll never bother you again.

Scene 13

(Dive shithole motel room)

(LOTTY slowly gets dressed as KEITH speaks into the motel phone.)

KEITH: *(Into phone)* Hey, um... Hey...Katherine, it's me, it's...it's Keith. If you're there, pick up. I'm sorry it's such an inappropriate hour, I...I'm sorry for a lotta shit. Look...This is shit, Kate. It's shit. How's Elizabeth? How was her party? I wish I was there, I...

(LOTTY has finished dressing.)

(She exits the motel room.)

(KEITH watches as she goes.)

(They do not make eye contact.)

KEITH: *(Into phone)* I'm not asking you to change your mind, I'm just... I love you both. *(Beat)* Sorry I called so late. *(He hangs up.)*

Scene 14

(The restaurant)

(JESSICA, still dolled-up, still alone, still waiting in vain.)

(10 seconds)

Scene 15

(The COLLIER's apartment)

(TRACIE turns on a light as she enters, a bouquet of flowers in her hand.)

(She looks around. No one)

TRACIE: Hello? Hello? Newton? Newt? April, Angie? *(She exits. Offstage)* Anybody home? Hello? It's

Mommy. Mommy's home. *(She re-enters. The flowers are now in a vase. She places the vase on a table. She picks up the mail.)*

(She sits in NEWTON'S *easy chair. She begins to look over the mail.)*

(She stops. She rests the mail in her lap. She looks around the quiet, empty apartment.)

(She looks through the mail once again.)

Scene 16

*(*GARY *and* LOTTY'S *home)*

*(*LOTTY'S *sitting alone on the love-seat.)*

(Silence)

*(*GARY *enters. He hangs his coat. He puts down his keys. He looks at his wife—she doesn't look back.)*

(He approaches.)

(Pause)

(He sits down beside her.)

(Pause)

(He gently places his hand on hers.)

(Pause)

(She turns her palm upward, into his palm.)

(They hold hands.)

(They don't speak.)

(They don't look at one another.)

*(*LOTTY *gently rests her head on* GARY'S *shoulder.)*

(Silence)

Scene 17

(The bar)

*(*KEITH *is on his stool, looking out.)*

*(*NEWTON *is also seated, looking out.)*

(A drink in front of each. Four barstools between them.)

(Silence)

(They are clearly aware of each other's presence, but there is no interaction. They sip their drinks.)

(Pause)

*(*KEITH *removes a pack of cigarettes from his shirt pocket. He removes a single cigarette. He replaces the pack into his pocket.)*

(He lifts a book of matches off the bar, strikes a match, lights his cigarette.)

(Silence)

(Eventually:)

NEWTON: Excuse me.

(No response)

NEWTON: Excuse me.

*(*KEITH *looks over.)*

NEWTON: Ya think I could get a smoke, maybe?

(Beat)

KEITH: You waitin' on someone? *(Beat)* Mmph? *(Beat)* Maybe I know 'em for ya.

NEWTON: I'm not waitin'.

KEITH: No?

NEWTON: No.

(Pause)

KEITH: I've never seen you in here. Maybe I know 'em.

NEWTON: Maybe not.

(Pause)

KEITH: I got menthol.

(KEITH removes the Newports.)

NEWTON: That's fine.

(Beat)

(KEITH slides NEWTON the pack of cigarettes. He then slides the book of matches. NEWTON lights a cigarette. He slips the book of matches into the pack and slides it back to KEITH.)

NEWTON: Thanks.

KEITH: Salud. *(He drinks.)*

(NEWTON drinks.)

(Long pause)

KEITH: You a cop? *(Beat)* Mmph? *(Beat)* Friend? *(Beat)* You the police?

(Beat)

NEWTON: Are you?

KEITH: No.

(Beat)

NEWTON: Neither am I.

(Beat)

(NEWTON looks away, straight ahead.)

(KEITH looks away, straight ahead.)

(Long pause)

KEITH: You got kids? Mmph? *(Beat)* How many? *(Beat)* I got one. A little girl. Betsy August Rose. *(Beat)* She was an accident. Maybe she was, maybe she wasn't. *(Pause)* But when she came? When she arrived, this little thing?

(Beat) All ya gotta do is walk through the door. *(Pause)*
I missed her 7th birthday party last week. I wasn't
invited. Her mother hates me. Maybe she does, maybe
she doesn't. Who knows?

(Silence)

(They drink.)

(They smoke.)

KEITH: *(Almost to himself)* [Salud.] *(Without looking over,*
he drinks.)

(NEWTON glances over. Then away.)

(Pause)

NEWTON: *(Almost to himself)* [Salud.] *(He drinks.)*

(Neither one looks to the other.)

(They smoke. They drink.)

(Long pause)

(Then music—Leonard Cohen's Alexandra Leaving*—from*
the beginning.)

(The song plays 10-15 seconds, then continues as:)

(Lights up on MISSY*—in the diner, behind the counter.*
She wears a waitress's apron and name-tag. She scrubs the
counter with a sponge. She fills a black plastic bin with dirty
cups, bowls, dishes.)

(She wipes sweat from her brow. She leans against the
counter. Exhausted, sad, her feet hurt. She continues
cleaning.)

(During the above: lights up on JESSICA*—in her small eat-*
in kitchen. In her nightshirt. A small TV glows. A teapot
whistles. She puts a tea-bag in a cup, she pours hot water.
She stirs. She puts the cup on the small kitchen table. She
pours a bowl of cereal. She pours milk into the bowl.)

(She sits at the table. She watches T V. She eats cereal. She
sips tea.)

(As JESSICA *sits at the table: lights on* LOTTY—*in her bedroom. She has one packed suitcase on the floor and a second partially-packed suitcase on a chair. She moves back and forth, from the bureau to the suitcase, filling it with clothes. She finishes filling the suitcase. She closes it. She puts it on the floor, next to the other suitcase. She looks around the bedroom. She sits, suitcases at her feet.)*

(As LOTTY *packs: lights on* GARY—*in a nice hotel room. Seated on the foot of the king-size bed. Wearing a black tuxedo.)*

(He takes off one shoe. Then the other. He takes off his socks and puts them in the shoes. He takes off his tux jacket, his bow-tie, his cummerbund.)

(He neatly drapes them over the back of a chair. He puts the shoes beneath the chair.)

(He untucks his shirt. He hesitates. He moves to the foot of the bed. He sits. He tries to make himself comfortable.)

(Lights on TRACIE—*in a bathroom. She wears a beautiful white wedding gown. She stares at herself in the mirror. Tears flow silently down her cheeks. She wipes them away. She composes herself. She stares at her reflection.)*

*(*NEWTON *and* KEITH *together at the bar.)*

*(*MISSY *alone in the diner.)*

*(*JESSICA *alone in her kitchen.)*

*(*LOTTY *alone in her bedroom.)*

*(*GARY *alone in the hotel room.)*

*(*TRACIE *opens the door of the bathroom. The door leads to the hotel room. She stands in the doorway.)*

*(*GARY *stands and faces her.)*

(Pause)

*(*TRACIE *slowly moves toward* GARY.*)*

(She stops 5-6 feet away.)

(They stare into each others' eyes—but do not touch, or move any closer.)

(The lights and music fade on every person, every location.)
(Silence)
(Blackness)

END OF PLAY